*The Johnson Foundation...*
*to help ideas to have...*
*on behalf of the common...*

*Our defining idea is con...*
*We believe that individual...*
*their ideas best flourish when...*
*nurtured by others. Those...*
*constitute communities of all kinds,...*
*communities which themselves...*
*nurturing...*

# THE JOHNSON FOUNDATION

> "Conferences seem a frail
> weapon to wield against
> formidable dragons like
> threats to peace and the
> neglect of children, but,
> well used, they have a
> power to instruct,
> motivate, and mobilize
> people for tasks that
> require attention."

*The Johnson Foundation's mission is
to help ideas to have consequences
on behalf of the common good.
Our defining idea is community.
We believe that individuals and
their ideas best flourish when
nurtured by others. Those "others"
constitute communities of all kinds,
communities which themselves
require nurturing.*

*Written by* CRAIG CANINE

# THE JOHNSON
# FOUNDATION

*The history of the people*

*who gathered in Wingspread*

*to talk and plan and dare to*

*make the world better.*

*Written by* CRAIG CANINE

THE JOHNSON FOUNDATION, INC.

*Racine, Wisconsin*

*Library of Congress Catalog Card Number:* 97-90638

ISBN 0-9641794-2-3

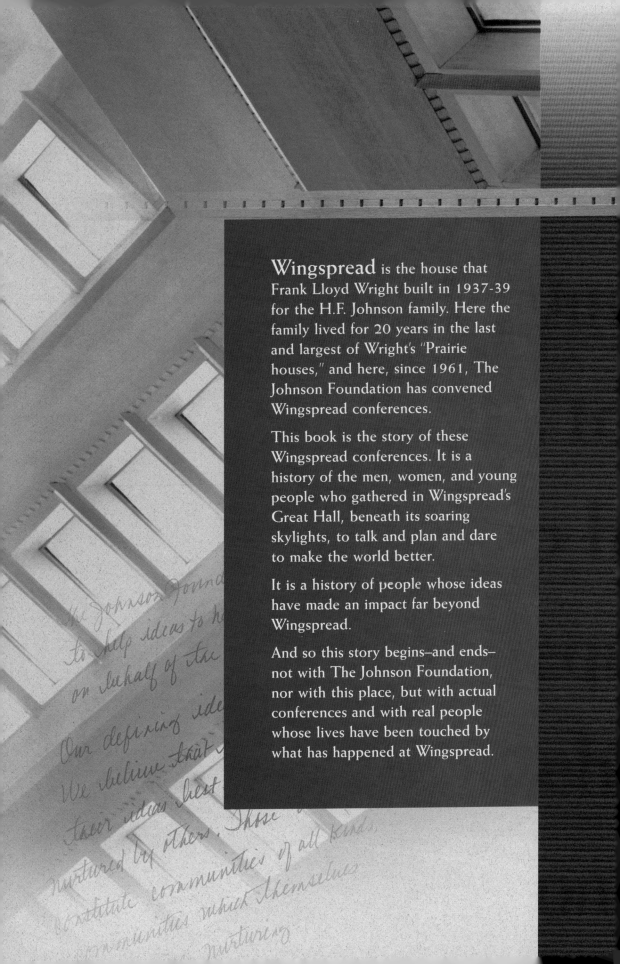

**Wingspread** is the house that Frank Lloyd Wright built in 1937-39 for the H.F. Johnson family. Here the family lived for 20 years in the last and largest of Wright's "Prairie houses," and here, since 1961, The Johnson Foundation has convened Wingspread conferences.

This book is the story of these Wingspread conferences. It is a history of the men, women, and young people who gathered in Wingspread's Great Hall, beneath its soaring skylights, to talk and plan and dare to make the world better.

It is a history of people whose ideas have made an impact far beyond Wingspread.

And so this story begins—and ends— not with The Johnson Foundation, nor with this place, but with actual conferences and with real people whose lives have been touched by what has happened at Wingspread.

On SUMMER NIGHTS, when the leafy neighborhoods of nearby Ann Arbor hum softly with locusts, the no-man's land behind Heather's apartment pops with gunfire. Drug dealers and their customers meet in the building across the street. Inside Heather's cinder-block building, a television echoes a pumped-up version of the tough neighborhood in Ypsilanti, Michigan, where Heather lives. Her baby son, Aaron, sleeps soundly in his bedroom. "I'm twenty-one now," Heather tells a visitor between drags on a Marlboro 100. "Sometimes I feel really young and sometimes I feel really old. Young because I haven't graduated from high school yet. A lot of other people my age have done so much that I haven't. I feel old because I'm a parent with a baby of my own. And I've been through a lot."

Heather grew up poor on the east side of Ann Arbor. Her father died when she was young. Her mother married a man who abused Heather, and her mother couldn't stop him. By the age of twelve, Heather—a petite, frail-looking little girl—was living on and off the streets. Soon she took up smoking, drinking, and experimenting with drugs. Heather's teachers wrote her off as a lost cause. On the rare occasions when she spoke, no one listened—except for a woman who ran a mentoring program from a tiny office in Heather's middle school. The woman, a teacher in the Ann Arbor public schools named Carol Tice, treated Heather with unaccustomed respect. So did the grandmotherly mentor who, through Carol's volunteer program, taught Heather how to make needlepoint crafts.

Slowly, Heather opened up. "I still feared for her life," Carol says, recalling those years. "The possibility of her destruction, whether at her own hand or someone else's, was always there. But in our little office at Heather's school, she seemed to find one place in the world where she felt safe and accepted."

Heather's life today is far from perfect, yet she feels happier than ever. Her apartment is neat and tidy. The newly painted walls are brightly decorated. "I'm more comfortable now," she says. "Even though I'm on AFDC, it's better than being on the street. I'd like to get my diploma so I can find a decent job. And I'd like my son to grow up with good educational opportunities, so he can be whatever he wants." She looks up and smiles.

"It may not look like much," she adds, "but this is a real improvement for me. Things are pretty good now."

When asked what has made this improvement in her life possible, Heather doesn't hesitate. "Carol and T-LC," she says, referring to Teaching-Learning Communities, the mentoring program Carol founded. "Carol has given me a lot in many ways."

Heather isn't the only one who has benefited from T-LC. Since Carol started the program in the early 1970s, thousands of children have participated in the program, which brings young people together with volunteer "grandparents" in school settings.

"It seems like a sweet, unobjectionable thing to do," Carol says. "But it can have a sharp edge—especially when it comes to working with at-risk adolescents who are dealing with major problems like drugs, gangs, teen pregnancy, and domestic violence. The intergenerational mentoring programs I'm involved in can bring a measure of healing to broken lives."

When asked to name her own sources of inspiration, Carol mentions the great anthropologist Margaret Mead, who helped her find her calling. In the same breath, Carol cites The Johnson Foundation and its conference center, a Frank Lloyd Wright landmark known as Wingspread. "If it hadn't been for Wingspread," she says, "I don't think I could have done my work. It's a model of the way people can be brought together in a forum of problem-solving and productive dialogue."

## A Conference Begins:
### October 22, 9:00 A.M.

*One recent autumn, Carol packed her bags and drove to the Detroit airport, bound for Milwaukee. Her final destination was a half-hour drive south of the airport. There, on a stubby finger of Wisconsin that juts into Lake Michigan, sits Wingspread. Carol was headed to The Johnson Foundation for a three-day meeting—her seventh or eighth Wingspread conference, she couldn't remember which. As she checked her bags in Detroit, she told a traveling companion,*

*Wingspread's "crow's nest" towers over the Great Hall roof.*

"I always feel a sense of excitement when I go to Wingspread. My experiences there have always been profound. I try to go feeling well-rested. The next forty-eight hours will be both exhausting and energizing—at least, if this conference lives up to the standard. And it's a very high standard. You'll see."

Carol first came to Wingspread in 1979. As a member of the U.S. National Commission on the International Year of the Child she travelled to Wingspread to prepare the Commission's report to President Carter. It was the end of a process that had begun with a meeting at the White House—a memorable setting, to be sure. At the later meeting in Wisconsin, Carol was surprised to find Wingspread just as memorable, in a different way. Wingspread's remote, sylvan setting promoted concentration. The conferees had the staff's undivided attention. Their every need was met, from local transportation arrangements and photocopying to fine meals, impeccably served. Beyond the logistic support, The Johnson Foundation's staff provided knowledgeable assistance in the field of children's advocacy. Carol met the Foundation's president, Leslie Paffrath. With his encouragement, she laid the groundwork for another Wingspread conference—a national gathering on educational programs that bring children and elderly adults together. The conference took place in the spring of 1980 and resulted in a report titled "Linking the Generations: Intergenerational Programs." Like many other reports of Wingspread conferences, it became a canonical document in its field. It still stands as an often-cited manifesto of the intergenerational movement.

Carol settled into her seat as the airplane took off and named several people who would be attending the imminent conference. "Some of them do not get along very well," she remarked. "It will be interesting to see if they can work with the group, or if they'll push their own agendas. Wingspread is a place where people have a chance to check their own agendas at the door and participate in a process for the greater good."

A humorist once remarked that "conferences are the leisure of the theoried class." That remark does not seem to apply to Wingspread, where the theoried class and the practical class "mix it up." Everything is organized around a single guiding principle: to help ideas to have consequences on behalf of the common good.

The process works a bit like honeybees in an apple orchard: the bees get nectar, the trees get pollinated, and, after a productive pause, society gets the apples.

"If I had to sum up Wingspread in one word, it would be multi-dimensional," Carol said. "One of its dimensions is the intellectual challenge of tackling a tough issue and taking it to the next level. That calls for a collection of the best minds in the field.

"And, there's the dimension of values. Wingspread provides a safe, neutral place to examine values and to articulate and clarify them, to express them in language and action-steps that put them to work in the world."

Carol Tice was not given to rapturous public outpourings. A woman of deep beliefs, affection, and intuition, she was above all reflective and serious. On the subject of Wingspread, though, she became expansive. Her destination that day was, for her, more than a place for good chat; it was a place where she expected to grow and be transformed.

"Another dimension of Wingspread would be continuity," she added. "The exact wording and focus of the Foundation's programs have changed over the years, but the overall emphases have remained stable: a civil, peaceful society both at home and abroad; healthy communities and families; productive education throughout the lifespan; and a sustainable human and natural environment. These have been strong themes from the Foundation's earliest years."

Wingspread conferences are all similar in some ways, she reflected, yet each one has its own character. "A Wingspread conference has a rigorous theoretical wholeness, with national scope and high ambitions," Carol said. "The program officers see to that, or your conference proposal isn't accepted. But when it is, you get the full Wingspread treatment"—world-class architecture, memorable food, courtly hospitality, and crisp logistic support. "What you make of an invitation to Wingspread, whether you're a convening organization or an individual conferee, is then completely up to you. You have at your disposal a wonderful atmosphere in which to ask the right questions. You don't always get all the answers while you're there, though. Often, the answers come later."

A Place to ask the right questions—
Wingspread was designed by Frank Lloyd
Wright as a home for Herbert F. Johnson, Jr.,
the fourth-generation leader of the Johnson
Wax Company. Shaped like a four-winged
pinwheel (the south wing is obscured by trees
in the aerial photo, *above*), the 14,000-square-
foot house balances grand spaces for
entertaining in the central Great Hall with
smaller, more intimate spaces in the bedroom
wings. The same features that made it an
inviting home also make it an ideal conference
center for The Johnson Foundation.

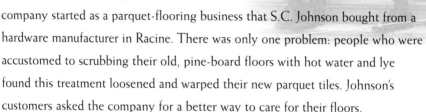

# A Corporate Adventure

In 1886, Samuel Curtis Johnson founded a company that would become the world's largest manufacturer of wax products. At first, however, it had nothing to do with wax. The company started as a parquet-flooring business that S.C. Johnson bought from a hardware manufacturer in Racine. There was only one problem: people who were accustomed to scrubbing their old, pine-board floors with hot water and lye found this treatment loosened and warped their new parquet tiles. Johnson's customers asked the company for a better way to care for their floors.

The company, which now included S.C. Johnson's son, Herbert Fisk Johnson, responded with thoughtful promptness. Knowing that the parquet floors of European castles had been maintained for centuries with waxes, the Johnsons looked into the matter. Their attention was soon drawn to the superior characteristics of a wax that came from the leaves of the carnauba palm tree, which grew in Brazil. The Johnsons formulated a carnauba-based paste wax and began to sell it as a sideline. Demand for floor wax increased faster than flooring sales did.

By 1910, the business, now called SC Johnson & Son, Inc., had nearly 100 employees. It shipped its last order of flooring in 1917 and concentrated on its former sidelines—floor waxes, wood finishes, and related items. Its popular consumer products made Johnson Wax a household name. The name spread internationally as the company added subsidiaries in England, Australia, Canada, and other countries.

Herbert Fisk Johnson, Jr., representing the third generation of Johnsons involved in the family business, assumed the company's leadership after his father died in 1928. Educated at Cornell University as a chemist, H.F. Johnson was a scientist as well as a businessman of unusual vision. The company, one of the first to adopt a forty-hour work week and paid holidays, expanded its progressive labor relations with profit-sharing in 1917. As the Great Depression persisted through the thirties, the company stuck to its commitment not to lay off employees. Instead of retrenching like many other companies, SC Johnson & Son stepped up both R&D and advertising, releasing new products that kept the company alive.

*Frank Lloyd Wright, left, and Herbert Fisk Johnson. Theirs has been described as a near-perfect collaboration of architect and client.*

In the midst of the business challenges of the 1930s, H.F. Johnson became absorbed in an issue that put him far ahead of his time. He wondered about the sustainability of the carnauba wax harvest in the rainforests of northeastern Brazil, the source of his company's most important raw material. To investigate the matter, he organized a research expedition, piloting the twin-engine Sikorsky flying boat himself.

In 1936, after his return to Racine, he published a short book about the experience. The book contained a statement of corporate environmental responsibility that was, in its day, practically unprecedented. "Until recent years," H.F. Johnson wrote, "American industry has used the raw materials employed in its manufactured products with little regard for future supply." He continued:

> **Forests were felled in haste,** mines stripped of the contents, the earth sucked dry of its treasures to provide necessities and luxuries for a lusty, growing nation. It was not until industry found itself embarrassed by actual shortages of raw materials that business began to recognize the need for scientific research at the source of supply of raw materials, or for technical research in the laboratory for synthetic materials to replace those which nature had once provided so bountifully.

The trip to Brazil represented a turning point for Johnson. He left home filled with questions about how to run the family company at a time of national economic crisis and rapid industrial change. He returned from Brazil with a solidified vision and plans for the future.

As a result, Johnson made a series of unusual yet decisive moves. In 1937 he established a philanthropic nonprofit trust, The Johnson Foundation. At about the same time, he commissioned Frank Lloyd Wright to design a new, expanded worldwide headquarters for the company. Shortly after that, he commissioned Wright to design a new house for his family.

Both the house and the corporate headquarters were hailed as architectural masterpieces. For Wright, the Johnson commissions represented a turning point after a dry spell in his tempestuous career. When asked what factor he considered most important in designing the Johnson Wax building, the architect made a

The massive masonry hearth stands at the center of the Great Hall, where conferees dine and assemble for large-group sessions. At the opposite end of the scale are small-group meeting places like that beneath the mezzanine, below. Wright varied the heights of floors and ceilings in the 40- by 60-foot room to create a hierarchy of visually distinct spaces.

comment that also applied to the house: "The human values involved. If you make men and women proud of their environment and happy to be where they are and give them some dignity and pride in their environment, it all comes out to the good where the product is concerned."

One important "product" of the house, which Wright called Wingspread because of its pinwheel-like floor plan, was H.F. Johnsons' two children, Karen and Samuel Curtis Johnson. They grew up at Wingspread, reveling in its ponds, woods, gardens, swimming pool, and crow's nest, which towered above the home's magnificent roofpeak.

By 1958, the family had lived in Wingspread for twenty years. Karen and Sam had flown the nest. H.F. Johnson and his wife decided to build another house next door, and to find other uses for Wingspread. A new nonprofit enterprise grew out of, and inherited the name of, the existing Johnson Foundation, while the wax company continued its philanthropic activities through another, separate entity. The new Johnson Foundation would benefit from the company's support, but it would constitute a distinct, philanthropic corporation with its own singular purpose: to operate Wingspread as an educational conference center devoted to the free exchange of constructive and purposeful ideas.

## DEVELOPING "READY MEN AND WOMEN"

A dedication ceremony to mark Wingspread's reopening as home of The Johnson Foundation took place in June 1961. On a sunny afternoon, H.F. Johnson donated his home formally to The Johnson Foundation. In doing so, he spoke of the new Foundation's purposes. "We will continue to promote educational excellence," he said. "We expect to continue to promote international understanding. We expect to promote intellectual and cultural growth. We expect to support our own overseas 'people-to-people' program."

He did not pretend that these areas of interest would insulate the Foundation from disagreement or conflict: "I should add," he said, "that we do not expect to run away from controversy, because it was from a mess of controversy that our forefathers evolved our democracy."

15

*Olgivanna Wright and H.F. Johnson, right, lead guests at the dedication of Wingspread.*

*Entering Wingspread through
the low-ceilinged main door,
below, then walking into the
Great Hall with its 30-foot-
high ceiling is like moving from
the vestibule into the nave of a
cathedral: the spirit soars.
Wright incorporated many
outdoor spaces—like the
cypress terrace, below left—
into Wingspread's design,
creating a sense of continuity
between indoors and out.*

The new Johnson Foundation was born at a time of national prosperity and optimism. The sunny mood at home, however, contrasted sharply with growing fears of impending global crisis. The prospect of war had assumed a new, nightmarish aspect since the nuclear bombings of Hiroshima and Nagasaki. Fueled by President Eisenhower's policy of "massive retaliation," America's nuclear arsenal quadrupled between 1953 and 1959.

In October 1957, the Soviet Union launched an intercontinental ballistic missile with a new kind of payload on board: a metal sphere containing two radio transmitters. The Soviets called the orbiting satellite Sputnik. As a psychological weapon of the Cold War, Sputnik had a devastating effect. Americans reacted with a sense of alarm bordering on panic. Who was to blame for this symbolic loss to the Communists? Admiral Hyman Rickover, who would become the father of the nuclear navy, blamed America's schools. As if to concur, the U.S. Office of Education published a report asserting that the United States had fallen far behind the Soviet Union in scientific and technical education.

Complacent assumptions no longer served as reliable guides; the need for new ideas and enlightened discussion had rarely seemed more urgent. H.F. Johnson, who had served as an advisor to the Eisenhower Administration, sensed the need for new venues where informed, purposeful discussion of vital issues could take place. In closing his remarks at Wingspread's dedication ceremony, he quoted the seventeenth-century English philosopher and statesman Francis Bacon, who once wrote that "Reading maketh a full man, conference a ready man, and writing an exact man."

"While we propose to do all three, here at Wingspread," H.F. Johnson said, "our main approach will be through conferences. Thus, in the words of Bacon, we intend to help develop more 'ready' men and women here. And in the spirit of Frank Lloyd Wright, we will also seek to stir and foster the creative nature of a free people, which is so enjoyable and, at the same time, so essential to their continued and expanding freedom."

The Johnson Foundation had its work cut out for it.

# The Early Years

H.F. Johnson began prospecting for candidates to lead the new foundation well before its formal founding. He learned of a young officer at the Carnegie Endowment for International Peace, Leslie Paffrath, who, among other responsibilities, had been in charge of the construction of the Carnegie building across from the new United Nations headquarters in New York City.

Johnson tapped Paffrath as an advisor during the early stages of organizing the as-yet embryonic foundation. Paffrath must have made a good impression. He soon realized he was being considered as a candidate to serve as the Foundation's first president.

While Paffrath had a good general sense of what The Johnson Foundation was to be, he had to put flesh on the bare bones now set before him. It was up to him to invent the new institution in its particulars. He had attended and convened scores of conferences during his career and had strong ideas about how it should be done. He was, to use Bacon's phrase, a ready man for the job.

Arriving with his family early in 1959, Paffrath sprang enthusiastically to his task. A Cold War crisis was brewing at the moment of his arrival. The previous fall, Soviet leader Nikita Krushchev had escalated international tensions with proclamations concerning Berlin, the partitioned city that was completely surrounded by Communist East Germany. Krushchev announced a May 27 deadline for the complete withdrawal of American troops from West Berlin. If the deadline wasn't met, the Soviet Union would sign a treaty with East Germany that would, in effect, close off American access to Berlin's Allied sector.

Acting quickly, Paffrath planned a briefing on the Berlin crisis and its international implications. The conversion of Wingspread to a conference center was not yet complete, so The Johnson Foundation's president asked officials of the University of Wisconsin–Extension Division if the conference could be held in Madison. Thus began a long and fruitful collaboration between The Johnson Foundation and the University of Wisconsin.

The Berlin Crisis conference took place only days before Krushchev's deadline.

*The Berlin Crisis conference was held in Madison, Wisconsin, in May 1959.*

A panel of foreign-policy specialists met in Madison with about fifty business and community leaders. One of the most prominent speakers at the conference was Hans Morgenthau, a political scientist whose views on the global balance of power carried tremendous weight in Washington. Morgenthau and others at the conference supported a policy of standing firm in West Berlin, yet without belligerent posturing or counterthreats.

Events in China had developed into another major international issue of the day. In 1959, U.S. relations with mainland China were in the deep-freeze. Chiang Kai-shek's Nationalist regime had fallen to Mao Tse-tung's communists in 1947, forcing Chiang to take refuge on the island of Taiwan. The U.S. government steadfastly recognized Taiwan as the one and only true China, refusing to acknowledge the People's Republic even after it became quite clear that the Communists were on the mainland to stay. Sino-U.S. relations were stuck at a dangerous dead end.

With the support of H.F. Johnson and the rest of The Johnson Foundation board, Paffrath leapt into these controversial waters. He suggested collaborating with the University of Cincinnati to hold a scholarly seminar on Sino-U.S. relations. This was a bold, politically dangerous thing to do in 1959. "It was less than ten years after the McCarthy period and the Korean War," recalled China expert Douglas Murray almost four decades later. In 1959, Murray was a young China scholar who, during the following decades, would convene or attend several Wingspread conferences on Sino-U.S. relations. "Back then," Murray added, "anti-communism still ran rampant. It wasn't safe to use the words 'People's Republic of China,' let alone advocate a better understanding of what was going on there. The people who attended the conference in 1959 were risking their reputations."

The mood of recrimination and denial concerning China ran so deeply that rational inquiry was effectively squelched. The Johnson Foundation offered an antidote to the suppression. The 1959 Cincinnati seminar was the first of nearly sixty conferences on China held under the Foundation's auspices, most of them at Wingspread, during the next thirty-five years. The list of specialists who attended these meetings reads like a "Who's Who" of contemporary China studies.

"Wingspread established itself as the meeting ground for a new, young generation of China scholars who are now the big names in the field," said Murray (who became one of those big names himself). "That in itself was an important thing."

In 1960, Paffrath plunged into another area of profound international concern. At a meeting in Chicago, he met Gerald Holton, a Harvard physicist who then served as editor of *Daedalus*, the highly respected journal of the American Academy of Arts and Sciences. Holton told Paffrath that he wanted to put out a special issue of *Daedalus* on arms control. He wanted to invite about twenty leading thinkers in the new field to contribute papers. The project would require a conference, to be held at the American Academy's headquarters in Cambridge, Massachusetts, for the purpose of discussing the problems of arms control and reviewing drafts of the papers. All that was lacking were the necessary funds.

With the Foundation's financial support, the arms-control conference was held and the resulting papers were published in the Fall 1960 issue of *Daedalus*. Contributors included Erich Fromm, Hubert Humphrey, Henry Kissinger, and Edward Teller. The special issue soon sold out; The Johnson Foundation sponsored a second printing. Those copies, too, quickly disappeared. A commercial publisher then acquired rights to the book and brought it before a wider audience under the title, *Arms Control, Disarmament and National Security*. It became a popular seller and a Book-of-the-Month Club selection. A reviewer for the *New York Times* called it "the bible of arms control."

"It was literally the first book on the subject," Paffrath recalled nearly forty years later. "There followed then a continuum of Wingspread meetings based on that book and the substance in it."

Even before Frank Lloyd Wright's masterpiece was available for public use, The Johnson Foundation had acquired a name for itself.

Among the first conferences of national scope held at Wingspread was a briefing on the United Nations. About forty business and civic leaders from the Midwest gathered at The Johnson Foundation's conference center in June 1961 to hear distinguished speakers address various aspects of the U.N. and its development. The speakers included Andrew Cordier, executive assistant to U.N. Secretary-

General Dag Hammarskjöld; and Brian Urquhart, one of the most respected senior members of the U.N.'s professional staff.

The most distinguished guest of all was Eleanor Roosevelt, who closed the U.N. conference with a featured address. Then seventy-seven years old and nearing the end of her life, Mrs. Roosevelt attended the Wingspread conference during her third and final stint as an active and influential U.N. official. Her talk was moved from Wingspread to Memorial Hall in downtown Racine, where larger numbers of townspeople could attend.

## THE FOUNDATION AND AFRICA

Distilled to its essence, The Johnson Foundation's purpose has always been to see that the right questions are asked. By helping to frame the right questions and bringing together forward-thinking minds to seek answers, the Foundation gained a reputation for addressing social issues long before the issues became headline news. An editorial writer for *The Milwaukee Journal* once told Paffrath that The Johnson Foundation served him as a kind of crystal ball. "Something that was always helpful to him as a journalist," Paffrath recounted, "was that he would look to the Foundation's list of upcoming conferences well in advance, and that way he could see what the issues were going to be several months, or even years, down the road." China was one such topic. Another was Africa.

Paffrath's interest in Africa dated back to his years at the Carnegie Endowment. At the Foundation, he cultivated acquaintances from among his Carnegie Endowment connections, including Frank Loescher, a Quaker from Philadelphia who made southern Africa his academic specialty and lifelong passion. Paffrath recruited Loescher to serve as a consultant to The Johnson Foundation. Loescher founded the United States-South Africa Leader Exchange Program, which the Foundation supported. South African clergymen, students, journalists, and scholars came to Wingspread to confer with American counterparts. This kind of exchange was almost as unheard of, at the time, as having visitors from China and the Soviet Union.

*Foundation President Leslie Paffrath, left, joins Eleanor Roosevelt and H.F. Johnson on the Wingspread grounds to plant a tree in honor of her visit.*

Starting in 1963, the Foundation supported a long series of Wingspread conferences on southern Africa. When the U.S. State Department finally devoted some attention to African matters, Wingspread stood ready to contribute. Secretary of State Henry Kissinger was preparing for talks with high-ranking South African officials when a Wingspread report on the future of Namibia (previously called South West Africa) made its way to his desk. Kissinger later said that he used the Wingspread report as a "working paper" in preparing for the talks and for his subsequent shuttle diplomacy in the region. The same Wingspread report was, in Paffrath's words, "viewed in South Africa as having been responsible for getting negotiations underway between the United Nations and the government of South Africa" after the U.N. barred South African delegates from the General Assembly. The negotiations led to a resolution that owed some part of its success to The Johnson Foundation.

## THE FOUNDATION AND THE ARTS

International understanding was, perhaps, the Foundation's preeminent program emphasis during its first two decades. This was by no means its only emphasis, however. Another one of the Foundation's stated program themes was "intellectual and cultural growth." This interest took lively form in the many lectures and concerts held at Wingspread for local audiences. It also took shape through conferences of national scope and impact, such as the 1962 Wingspread Conference on the Arts.

Some eighty participants, including professional artists, arts administrators, critics, and scholars of the arts, gathered at Wingspread to consider ways of fostering the arts in America. Among the conferees were philosopher and literary critic Kenneth Burke, modern-dance master Merce Cunningham, man of letters Gilbert Seldes, Pulitzer-prize-winning poet Karl Shapiro, and novelist Glenway Westcott.

The conferees, despite their wide-ranging views, managed to agree on one thing: the federal government should assume a more active role as a patron of the arts across the United States. To promote this view in a concrete and immediate way,

*The idea for the National Endowment for the Arts was born at Wingspread.*

the group resolved to send a telegram to President John Kennedy at the White House. This (in part) is what the telegram said:

## Eighty participants in the Wingspread Conference

on the Arts, assembled in Racine, Wisconsin, representing a wide cross-section of American art leadership and endeavor, passed a unanimous resolution at its concluding session, that you be respectfully petitioned to proceed as soon as possible toward the organization of a great national conference in Washington, D.C., for the purpose of examining the condition and future of the arts in America.

The telegram to the White House was only a start. The Foundation provided funds to increase the print run of the issue of *Arts in Society* that reported the Wingspread arts conference. Paffrath and his staff sent copies to scores of influential people in Washington. Notes of appreciation came back to the Foundation from many recipients including Jacqueline Kennedy's social secretary, Letitia Baldrige, who wrote that "Mrs. Kennedy took this report with her to Florida for the Easter holiday, and I know she will be very interested in its contents."

Whether Mrs. Kennedy read it or not, the First Couple certainly brought a heightened sense of appreciation for the arts to the White House. Soon after John Kennedy was elected, he became the first President to appoint a special White House Consultant on the Arts. The initial holder of this position was August Heckscher, whose respected assistant, Barbara Donald, had attended the Wingspread arts conference. She had Heckscher's ear, and Heckscher had the President's.

Some months after the conference, Heckscher submitted a report to President Kennedy that recommended the establishment of a presidential council on the arts and spoke of the need for a federal "Arts Foundation." Kennedy asked Congress for action on a bill that would have turned some of Heckscher's recommendations into law. Congress ignored the President's requests. So, on June 12, 1963—almost exactly a year after the Wingspread Conference on the Arts took place—Kennedy took the unusual step of issuing an executive order (not subject to Congressional approval) creating a President's Advisory Council on the Arts. On November 22, 1963, a story in the *New York Times* reported that appointment of the Arts Council was imminent. That same day, in Dallas, President Kennedy was assassinated. His executive order was never implemented.

As President, Lyndon Johnson repeated Kennedy's call for establishment of a National Arts Council. Opposing forces in Congress succumbed and the Council was created in August 1964. The following year, 1965, Congress passed the National Foundation on the Arts and the Humanities Act. The bill established both the National Endowment for the Humanities and the National Endowment for the Arts.

## LAUNCHING PUBLIC RADIO

If the U.S. government's role in the creative arts was at a crossroads in the 1960s, so was its role in noncommercial broadcasting. The dramatic rise of television as a cultural force during the fifties and early sixties had left two victims in its wake: radio and educational television.

In 1965, a newly formed Carnegie Commission on Educational Television began a two-year project that culminated in the report *Public Television: A Program for Action*. This influential publication set forth a vision for public broadcasting that went beyond routine instructional fare. Public broadcasting would address "all that is of human interest and importance" that commercial broadcasting would not or could not support.

President Johnson urged Congress to enact legislation based on the Carnegie report. The resulting bill became known as the Public Television Act of 1967. It was a great moment in the history of creative television, but radio had been left out in the cold.

In its heyday, of course, radio had proven its transfixing powers to inform, entertain, and transport the imagination. But the art and craft of creative radio broadcasting had gone underground. It survived in a few scattered places, championed mainly by students and devotees of Edward R. Murrow. One of Murrow's disciples was Jerrold Sandler, director of National Educational Radio, a division of the National Association of Educational Broadcasters. The NAEB kept noncommercial radio alive during the period, from the late thirties through the fifties, when educational stations were dropping off the airwaves by the score.

There might well have been no public radio at all, however, if Sandler and his NAEB colleagues hadn't rallied supporters to the cause. Just as the Carnegie Commission on Educational Television was beginning its work, Sandler communicated with The Johnson Foundation about holding a national conference on educational radio at Wingspread. It seemed a propitious place to hold such a conference. Wingspread had, by the mid-sixties, already acquired an aura of prestige. The public television report would bear the Carnegie stamp; the radio conference would bear the imprimatur of Wingspread and The Johnson Foundation.

The conference, titled "Educational Radio as a National Resource," took place over three days in September 1966. By all accounts, it was a resounding success, providing supporters of public radio with a set of specific action steps with which to pursue their goals.

The most immediate challenge was to convince members of Congress that radio deserved equal billing with TV in the pending Public Television Act. "Make no mistake about it," Sandler stated before a Senate subcommittee, "radio is *not* merely television without pictures." Paffrath also testified before Congress, urging that the words "and radio" be added everywhere the word "television" appeared in the original bill.

Congress passed an amended bill, which was titled "the Public Broadcasting Act." In it, radio shared equal standing with television. The bill authorized creation of the Corporation for Public Broadcasting to act as a funding and policy-making agency. CPB, in turn, created the Public Broadcasting Service for television in 1969. National Public Radio emerged from CPB several months later, and was incorporated in February 1970.

A decade later, the manager of WHA Radio in Madison, Wisconsin—a station often cited as an early model of what public radio could be—sent a letter to The Johnson Foundation. "As you know," the station manager wrote, "the Wingspread conference on educational radio in the 1960s paved the way for radio's inclusion in the Public Broadcasting Act of 1967."

## The Wingspread Way:
### October 22, 5:30 P.M.

At 5:30 P.M. on Tuesday, October 22, Carol Tice and her fellow conferees
boarded a bus at the Racine Marriott for the fifteen-minute ride to Wingspread.
The bus was filled with eager chatter—the sounds of people meeting for the first
time mixed with the sounds of old friends reuniting. The thirty-five people on
board represented a powerful reservoir of energy.

After saying a round of hellos, Carol settled into her seat and watched the
passing autumn scenery. The bus turned onto a quiet road lined, on one side,
with estate homes and, on the other, the lapping waves of Lake Michigan. A few
moments later, it passed through the Wingspread gate and headed down a long,
gently curving driveway.

Carol stayed in her seat while the bus unloaded. "I get excited when I'm here
because of all that Wingspread has come to mean to me," she said. "There's such
a strong sense of place here. It's like an anchor. Everything at Wingspread helps
and encourages you to focus on the work at hand." Her gaze fixed on the Frank
Lloyd Wright building. "Even the architecture adds to the effect. When you go
into Wingspread, the experience has the capacity to transform. Part of it is the
warm tones, the wood, the fireplaces. Even in summer, when the fireplaces are idle,
the hearths project a warm, tranquil quality. The atmosphere invites reflection,
but not passive reflection. The unusual design of the house is an ever-present
reminder that new thought is possible."

Countless visitors have made similar observations. Charles Bray, president of
The Johnson Foundation for the decade beginning in 1988, recalled one instance
in particular. He was standing in the building's great central hall welcoming a
newly arrived conference. As he made his remarks, he noticed that one member of
the group—a Native American—was paying little attention. The man was
concentrating, instead, on the building. He walked slowly, almost ceremoniously,
around the room, pausing at intervals. After Bray had finished speaking, the
man approached him and announced emphatically, "This place has spirit."

A more recent guest—the president of a national land-conservation organization—sent The Johnson Foundation staff an appreciative note after attending a 1996 conference. "We came, we saw, and our spirits soared," he wrote. "The setting of Wingspread was absolutely transformational."

Insiders sometimes refer to the Foundation's philosophy as "the Wingspread Way." It might also be called "The Tao of Conferencing—Wingspread Style." Bray summed it up as "The Johnson Foundation's unending effort to achieve perfection in every detail."

The process gets a tune-up after every conference, when the relevant staff members get together for quick consideration of two logistic questions (judgments of conference impact take longer to gestate). The questions are: "How did we do?" and "How could we have done better?"

"If you don't pay attention to the details," Bray said, "then the overall quality of things will begin to deteriorate. All of a sudden you'll show up on a Monday morning and the place will have changed, and it will be very hard to pull it back together again. Sweating the details is what makes the Marines—and Wingspread—different."

In spite of all the experience and planning that go into Wingspread conferences, each one is a new experiment in human dynamics. Every conference contains, at the outset, the seeds of both success and failure. When one fails, it is frequently because the convening group's leaders failed to respond flexibly to signs of trouble as their conference unfolded. The Foundation's program officers are there to help, but only if help is sought.

Even the most successful conferences often look as if they're headed for disaster until the very end. And some, of course, never recover; not every human venture succeeds. A certain amount of conflict and respectful disagreement are vital to productive outcomes. Conference leaders face the nerve-racking challenge of striking a balance between control and chaos, structure and improvisation. "It's scary to be in a room for three days with high-powered people, not knowing exactly what the outcome will be," Carol observed on opening night. "As a conference leader or participant, you have to take some risks. But Wingspread provides such a supportive environment that the odds are rigged in your favor."

The Great Hall of Wingspread.

The Johnson Foundation provides such an environment, in part, by seeking its own balance between the need for productive ritual and continuity, on the one hand, and the need for reevaluation and change, on the other. By the late 1970s, it had reached a moment in its own history when the balance called for change. Paffrath had been the Foundation's president for nearly twenty years and was approaching his sixty-fifth birthday. Wingspread was well established both as a conference center and as an agent of socially responsible change. The scope of its activities was extremely wide, though it was perhaps best known for its work in promoting peace, productive communication, and democratic reform throughout the world.

To see the Foundation's many programs through, Paffrath had assembled a core group of extremely capable staff members. Like newspaper reporters, the Foundation's program officers tended to be astute generalists with assigned "beats." Rita Goodman joined the staff as a program officer in 1962 with responsibilities mainly in women's issues and international affairs. Paffrath hired Henry Halsted ten years later to cultivate the Foundation's programs in education, the media, and the arts. Richard Kinch came aboard in 1976 to assume a program portfolio in race relations, criminal justice, and community development. A small administrative staff kept the facility running smoothly.

## A WIDER VOICE:
### "CONVERSATIONS FROM WINGSPREAD"

Countless people all over the country knew Wingspread not because of its conferences, but because of outreach programs that were launched during the Paffrath era. Chief among these was "Conversations from Wingspread," a long-running series of weekly radio programs. The programs took advantage of the parade of distinguished experts who passed through Wingspread to attend conferences. Nearly 200, mostly commercial radio stations, broadcast the syndicated series to listeners in all fifty states from 1972 through 1988. Featured guests and topics included Marshall Shulman on U.S.-Soviet relations, Henry Steele Commager on the study of history, Coretta Scott King and William Julius Wilson on race, John V. Lindsay on city government, David Brower on ecology

*Producer John Yoder with Coretta Scott King, one of many guests on the radio program "Conversations from Wingspread."*

and the energy crisis, William Raspberry (who later became a Johnson Foundation trustee) on black journalism, Madeleine L'Engle on art and religion, Jesse Jackson on education in America, Hans Bethe on nuclear power, and Buckminster Fuller on just about everything. "Conversations from Wingspread" won a number of awards, including a George Foster Peabody Award, the Oscar of radio.

The prime mover behind "Conversations from Wingspread" was Melvin Brorby, an especially active member of the Foundation's board of trustees. Brorby was a founding partner in a Chicago advertising agency which eventually became one of the world's largest marketing communications agencies. He advised successive generations of Johnsons on SC Johnson & Son's advertising strategy. Brorby also launched the idea for a Wingspread Fellows Program (renamed the Melvin Brorby Wingspread Fellows Program following his death in 1996 at the age of 101) which brings outstanding students from Midwest colleges to observe and learn from Wingspread conferences.

## A New President

All this was in place when Paffrath officially retired from the presidency in mid-1980. His successor was William B. Boyd. With a doctorate in European diplomatic history, Boyd came to The Johnson Foundation from the presidency of the University of Oregon, where he had served since 1975. His previous academic posts included a vice-chancellorship at the University of California, Berkeley, from 1966 to 1968, during the height of student unrest.

The world in 1980 was a different place than it had been twenty years before, when Wingspread was converted from a residence to an institution. By 1980, the debacles of Vietnam and Watergate, a protracted energy shortage, high inflation combined with economic stagnation, and a heightened awareness of environmental degradation, contributed to a national crisis of confidence.

The Johnson Foundation, too, shifted in focus. Its mission remained the same, but its program guidelines became somewhat more specific. The overall distribution of resources moved perceptibly away from the theme of international understanding and toward educational excellence and "Improvement of the

Human Environment"—a phrase that, in practice, referred mainly
to domestic social and environmental programs.

"When I arrived," Boyd recalls, "The Johnson Foundation was strongly associated
with arms control, the U.N., and other broad, peace-oriented things. Its business
was bringing good minds together and focusing them on worthwhile projects and
hoping that out of this, a force would be mobilized. It was a very appealing thought.

"By the time I came here, though," he continued, "things like arms control had
passed the point where an organization like The Johnson Foundation could make
a contribution. As our role in that decreased, however, Rita Goodman continued
to put together effective conferences that addressed U.S.-Soviet and U.S.-
China relations."

Along with adopting a somewhat narrower and more domestic focus, Boyd hoped
to re-energize the Foundation as a generator of its own conference initiatives.
Ideas for Wingspread conferences had always come from a variety of sources,
including the Foundation's staff and board of trustees. In the late 1970s, however,
the dominant operating mode was more reactive than proactive. "I tried to get
beyond the idea that we were only here to respond to other peoples' ideas," Boyd
said years later. "Instead, I hoped to develop a more coherent agenda of our own
and to seek collaborations with partners who were interested in pursuing that
agenda with us."

## IN AT THE BEGINNING:
## A REFINED FOCUS

Among the most visible outcomes of the many collaborations formed during this
period was the launch of the Domestic Policy Association. The DPA, which
adapted its name and mission from the highly esteemed Foreign Policy
Association, took shape during a series of Wingspread conferences jointly
sponsored by The Johnson Foundation and the Charles F. Kettering Foundation.

The DPA's purpose was to encourage informed citizens to assemble and discuss
pressing national issues. The DPA would produce nonpartisan materials that

*William B. Boyd, second president of the Foundation, brought a renewed focus on education.*

would help educate people on selected issues, provide forums for their discussion, and then inform elected officials of the considered judgments of the citizen-participants.

The DPA's discussion programs, subsequently renamed National Issues Forums, celebrated their fifteenth anniversary in 1997. These forums were "not another symposium for expert opinion, nor occasions for partisan politics," explained David Mathews, president of the Kettering Foundation and Secretary of Health, Education, and Welfare during the Ford administration. "Like the old town meetings, the DPA provides forums in which concerned citizens can discuss public issues, air their differences, think them through, and work toward acceptable solutions."

Issues involving women and minorities, which had always attracted plenty of interest at Wingspread, became even more prominent during William Boyd's presidency. In 1983, for example, a small but representative group of prominent women gathered at Wingspread to discuss the future of the women's movement. The following spring, women from Europe, the Caribbean, the Third World, and North America converged at Wingspread for the U.S.-based meeting in a series of three planning sessions (the others were held at equally world-famous conference centers in Bellagio, Italy, and Ditchley Park, England) for the impending United Nations World Conference on Women.

A group of African-American civil-rights leaders and scholars, including Jesse Jackson, Coretta Scott King, Eleanor Holmes Norton, Roger Wilkins, and Eddie N. Williams, met at Wingspread in 1983 to discuss African-American priorities for the 1980s. Native Americans also met at Wingspread on many occasions during the 1970s and 1980s to discuss a range of conference topics, such as fighting anti-Indian prejudice, preserving native arts, and improving tribal governance.

Children and youth emerged during the 1980s as a focus of increasing interest and concern at The Johnson Foundation. Program Officer Richard Kinch formed alliances with social-service agencies and organizations that sought remedies for the increasingly serious problems of childhood poverty, teen pregnancy, and child abuse. Although these issues are all too familiar now, they had not yet

*Planning sessions for the United Nations World Conference on Women were held at Wingspread.*

become matters of broad public awareness when The Johnson Foundation first became involved.

"When I arrived at The Johnson Foundation," Boyd recalled, "I had not heard the term child abuse. It was not yet in the current of everyday thinking. Yet now there's an enormous concentration of concern and energy and money devoted to protecting children from abuse and neglect. I think that Dick Kinch started a chain of activity that gave the idea more currency and got more people thinking about it. And, of course, you can't separate the child from the family, so youth and family became an increasingly important line of thought at The Johnson Foundation."

Of all the important lines of thought that converged at Wingspread, education became the most important of all. "My intellectual interests had shifted to precollegiate education," Boyd explained. "Henry Halsted was education officer, but he was primarily engaged in higher education. The program guidelines were sufficiently wide that there was room for me to pursue education at the primary and secondary levels."

When Boyd started pursuing these interests every thoughtful observer of American education already knew that public high schools were in trouble. By mid-1983, nearly thirty major studies on aspects of the problems plaguing American precollegiate education had either recently come out or were nearing completion. "Not since Sputnik had schools been the center of such interest," Boyd wrote later. Given this intensity of expert attention, what could The Johnson Foundation contribute? The last thing needed, Boyd realized, was another report. What was needed, however, was a venue, a convening force that could bring the best minds in the field together to exchange views and develop a stronger consensus about exactly what was broken and how to fix it.

The Johnson Foundation joined the efforts of a number of foundations and associations to improve secondary education. The *Wingspread Journal*, a publication that the Foundation began to publish in 1980, carried feature stories in every issue about major education conferences that had recently taken place at Wingspread. Some of the country's leading authorities on primary and secondary education,

Like most good conferences, Wingspread encourages and rewards sustained attention both to the big picture and the details. Its sculpted spaces, carved dentils, unusual masonry work and tiered ranks of skylights all contribute to a rich, multi-dimensional whole.

including Ernest Boyer and Theodore Sizer, became repeat visitors to Wingspread. Deans of education from about forty of the nation's top research universities began meeting regularly at Wingspread to discuss sweeping changes in teacher education and in professional standards for teachers. This consortium of university deans called itself the Holmes Group in honor of Henry Holmes, a former dean of Harvard University's Graduate School of Education.

Patricia Albjerg Graham, one of Holmes' successors at Harvard and a veteran Wingspread conferee, joined The Johnson Foundation's board of trustees in 1983—the same year the Holmes Group began its series of Wingspread conferences. "Wingspread helped get the conversation going about what needed to be done to improve education in America," Graham recalled years later. There was a great deal of activity in the field throughout the 1980s, she added, but "Wingspread was absolutely in at the beginning."

## Breakdown:
### October 23, 8:30 A.M.

*Wednesday, October 23, dawned cloudy but rainless. The night had been windy and wet, but morning held the equivocal promise of a day that could turn either sunny or stormy. On the bus to Wingspread, which left the hotel at 8:30 A.M., the atmosphere hung thick with a sense of contrasting possibilities for the day.*

*The morning began with two speeches, then conferees broke into work groups, which met in separate spaces to brainstorm. After this session, everyone reassembled to generate ideas.*

*By noon, a subterranean river of discontent broke through to the surface. The conference had reached its halfway point, and many members of the group still felt bogged down in abstract preliminaries. Matters did not improve after lunch, as conferees saw time slip away. A few minutes before 3:00 P.M., Carol passed a note to an observer sitting next to her. "I feel that we are running out of time and may not get to any practical intergenerational agenda," her note said. "I will be amazed at this point if we come up with something."*

*The north wing of Wingspread with its cantilevered porch and balcony.*

*Across the driveway, Charles Bray was working in his office when he heard that the conference had reached a crisis point. He smiled. "That's an almost universal experience," he said. "There's usually a moment in the afternoon of the second day of a conference when the group reaches a breakdown point. It tends to come right at 3:00 P.M., give or take ten minutes. It can be a salutary phenomenon. It means people at the conference care and that they'll make a special effort to achieve a positive outcome.*

*"It's a very Jeffersonian process," Bray added. "Jefferson knew that a deliberative democracy, when functioning properly, would occasionally get a bit messy."*

## THE THIRD DECADE

June 1988 marked another major transition for The Johnson Foundation. William Boyd and five other staff members, including veteran program officers Rita Goodman and Henry Halsted, retired.

Boyd's successor, Charles W. Bray, came to The Johnson Foundation following a thirty-year career in diplomacy and foreign service. He had served as chief press spokesman for the Department of State during Richard Nixon's presidency. Under the Carter administration, Bray became the first career public servant to be appointed Deputy Director of the U.S. Information Agency. He served as American Ambassador to Senegal from 1981 to 1985.

Bray's background suggested that The Johnson Foundation might, under his leadership, adopt a renewed emphasis on international affairs. That didn't happen. "Not only did it not happen," Bray said in retrospect, "but we became less focused on foreign policy in our programs." He went on to cite some reasons for this. First, he said, his previous experience made him acutely aware of how resistant the White House and State Department were to ideas from outside the Washington Beltway. Secondly, the late 1980s saw the sudden dissolution of the Soviet Union. "When we took down the scaffolding of the Cold War," Bray recalled later, "we discovered that our own society was in real trouble. At this historic moment of American *perestroika*, The Johnson Foundation had an opportunity to make a difference by helping to rebuild and strengthen our own communities."

Wright believed that a heightened experience of nature led to a better understanding of one's own, inner nature. He designed Wingspread to encourage the awareness and cultivation of both. Foundation and company Chairman Samuel C. Johnson confers with Johnson Foundation President Charles Bray, below.

With Bray at the helm, The Johnson Foundation did not so much alter its direction as it underwent a refitting, the better to accomplish its historic purposes in re-imagined ways. Its new guidelines, for example, contained an explicit statement of the Foundation's historic interest in, and support for, its own community, both locally and regionally. And, they described the purposes of the Keland Endowment Fund. Karen Johnson Keland (H.F. Johnson's daughter) and her children established this separate resource within The Johnson Foundation to support Wingspread conferences in three distinct areas: promotion of the arts; assistance to people having physical, developmental, or mental disabilities; and preservation of the environment.

## THE ENVIRONMENT AND THE GREAT LAKES

The perfect Wingspread conference or series of conferences would somehow combine every one of the Foundation's program interests—which were still wide-ranging—in a single subject that was ripe for effective action. One topic that came close to this ideal in the 1980s was the health of the Great Lakes basin. This was a matter of international environmental concern, of course, since it affected both Canada and the United States. Great Lakes pollution caused economic and health problems that threatened communities, families, and children in both countries. Implementing solutions required the coordinated efforts of institutions of science, health, regulation, enforcement, conservation, and public policy. The whole enterprise was full of educational opportunities. Plus, it hit close to home for residents of Racine and southeastern Wisconsin, living as they do on the western shore of Lake Michigan.

The issue of Great Lakes pollution was by no means new to the public, nor was it new to The Johnson Foundation. Throughout the seventies and eighties, the Foundation hosted Wingspread conferences on topics such as "The Future of the St. Lawrence Seaway," "Preservation of Lake Michigan," and "Pollution Abatement Strategies for the Great Lakes."

By 1990, the Great Lakes looked almost pristine compared with their visibly wretched condition a few decades before. Yet signs of trouble lingered. PCBs, DDT, and a panoply of other synthetic chemicals circulated in Great Lakes' ecosystems. Fish, birds, and mammals continued to exhibit severe physical abnormalities—a stark warning that health risks can persist years after direct discharges cease.

The Johnson Foundation's program staff saw an opportunity for re-invigorated action on the issue. They pursued it by forming collaborative relationships with a variety of organizations, including the U.S. Environmental Protection Agency, the Council of Great Lakes Governors, the Environmental Defense Fund, the World Wildlife Fund, and the International Joint Commission, a binational organization established in 1909 to advise Canada and the United States on issues affecting the two countries' common border. Collaborations like these generated nearly twenty conferences on various Great Lakes environmental issues from 1990 to 1995.

That conferences beget conferences is an often-noted fact of life at The Johnson Foundation. A good example of this phenomenon stemmed from the Foundation's work on cleaning up the Great Lakes environment. A pioneering zoologist named Theo Colborn, who worked as a senior scientist at the World Wildlife Fund, knew about the Foundation's contributions in this area.

Colborn's research interest, as Vice President Al Gore wrote, in the mid-1990's, took up where Rachel Carson's work left off. Whereas Carson brought worldwide attention to the ability of certain pesticides and other chemical pollutants to cause cancer, Colborn began to show that some of the same chemicals (DDT, PCBs, and others) exerted hormone-like effects on animals' endocrine systems. Colborn amassed a long and growing list of wildlife studies that documented an array of reproductive anomalies, including shrunken sexual organs, reduced sperm counts, drops in birth rates, and sudden disappearances of entire animal populations.

To determine whether some of these chemically induced reproductive alterations were affecting not just wildlife, but also humans, Colborn and the World Wildlife Fund invited a group of experts in endocrinology, immunology, toxicology, wildlife management, zoology, and other disciplines to Wingspread in July 1991. As this multinational group of experts compared data from their respective fields of specialty, a bigger picture took shape.

*John Peterson Myers and Theo Colborn at a Wingspread conference on hormone-disrupting chemicals.*

Colborn and two collaborators—Dianne Dumanoski and John Peterson Myers—described this alarming picture and the process leading to its emergence in a book titled *Our Stolen Future: Are we threatening our fertility, intelligence, and survival?—A scientific detective story* (Dutton, 1996). The *New York Times Book Review* cited *Our Stolen Future*—a work born in four Wingspread conferences held over four years—as a notable book of 1996.

If Great Lakes ecosystems still faced intractable problems in the 1990s, so did American education. The Holmes Group, meeting at Wingspread in the mid-1980s, devised strategies for improving the quality of education for high-school and primary-school teachers. Another group of scholars, chaired by Arthur Chickering and Zelda Gamson, met at Wingspread in 1986 to ask what could be done to improve the general quality of teaching at the college level. Participants at this conference sought to identify key principles that characterized the most educationally successful institutions of higher learning. They created a statement that was published in an article in the American Association of Higher Education (AAHE) *Bulletin* as the "Seven Principles for Good Practice in Undergraduate Education."

The article, written by Chickering and Gamson, recognized that college faculty—who are usually hired for their scholarly and research credentials—might welcome some help with their teaching skills. In simple, jargon-free language, the Wingspread "Seven Principles" distilled effective undergraduate teaching into a series of practical ideas, each supported by a brief explanation and a few examples.

With encouragement from the AAHE, The Johnson Foundation made the "Seven Principles" more widely available. "We reprinted the piece as an insert in the Summer 1987 *Wingspread Journal*," recalled Susan Poulsen, then The Johnson Foundation's director of communications. "We also printed 10,000 copies of the insert to send out to anyone who requested one. I thought that was a ridiculously high number. But they were gone in days. During the next ten years we printed another 200,000 copies, and they've all gone like hotcakes. Clearly, they met a need."

In 1989, the Foundation identified science and technology education as a major program emphasis. During the next few years, it cultivated and hosted nearly thirty Wingspread conferences on this theme. The Foundation also supported conferences devoted to early childhood education, to ideas like "values education" and "experiential education," to the special challenges of inner-city schools, and to restructured institutions such as charter schools.

Conferences in all these areas often helped convening groups to secure major grants from other sources for further work. Coming, as it usually did, at a crucial time and in a unique way, The Johnson Foundation's support often had a multiplier effect. Wingspread conferences on science education, for example, helped convening organizations secure major foundation and government grants worth more than $70 million. Those on service learning helped generate more than $100 million.

Perhaps the Foundation's single most ambitious undertaking during the Bray era was an initiative addressing the need for restructuring American higher education. In January 1993, Bray asked William Brock—a former congressman, senator, Chairman of the Republican Party, U.S. Trade Representative, and Secretary of Labor—to chair a committee to examine the question, "What does society need from higher education?"

Brock and the project's sponsors, which included The Johnson Foundation, The William and Flora Hewlett Foundation, Lilly Endowment Inc., and The Pew Charitable Trusts, recruited sixteen people to serve on what came to be called the Wingspread Group on Higher Education. The group met monthly at Wingspread for much of 1993 to produce a statement that would guide a movement to hold American higher education to a higher standard of performance in meeting the needs of society.

One of the group's members was Gilbert Amelio who, in 1993, held the titles of chairman and CEO at National Semiconductor Corporation. Amelio had maintained a long-standing interest in trying to make American universities more responsive to the needs of the businesses that eventually hired most of the graduates. "There was a huge disconnect between what we knew were good educational practices versus what was really happening on campuses," said Amelio.

*In 1993, William Brock led The Wingspread Group on Higher Education.*

Wingspread's unexpected features, from the rooftop "crows nest" and the long cantilevered balcony to the lozenge-shaped masonry planters and the sculpture collection, all help to remind conferees that creative thought is possible. Its garden paths and wooded trails invite reflection.

The project resulted in a report called *An American Imperative: Higher Expectations for Higher Education*. Colleges and universities, the report said, "must educate more people, and educate them far better. That will require new ways of thinking. Given the diversity of American higher education, there can be no single formula for change common to all, but we do believe that there are at least three fundamental issues common to all 3,400 colleges and universities: taking values seriously; putting student learning first; [and] creating a nation of learners."

Some 25,000 copies of *An American Imperative* were printed, distributed, and sold. In a nation that often seems sated with reports and high-minded rhetoric, *An American Imperative* rose quietly but persistently to the top in the following years. It was read, remembered, and discussed. The Wingspread report had a bellwether quality: many of the ideas it proposed gained greater currency in the national discourse on higher education.

"I think The Wingspread Group made a big difference," Amelio said. "I've talked to countless people on the university side who have read the report and praised its contribution. Beyond that, many university deans and presidents have said, 'We're adopting this as a guideline,' which is what we had hoped for. The linkages between the report and its effects are subtle, but it was clearly a landmark effort, widely seen as a strong step in the right direction."

## Running Out of Time:
### Day 2, 4:00 P.M.

*Following the afternoon's crisis, things started to come together. A 4:00 P.M. refreshment break helped to calm nerves and focus minds. When the group reconvened, participants went at it with a zeal compounded by twenty-four hours of restless anticipation. Before long, the group had mapped out a skeletal action plan.*

*During dinner, many conferees felt that the group had indeed turned a corner. They were optimistic about heading home the next afternoon with an action agenda that would prove useful to the organizations they represented. Others weren't so sure.*

*Catherine Milton tended toward this point of view.*

*Wingspread seems "integral with its setting," born of the prairie.*

# AN INCUBATOR FOR YOUTH SERVICE

Catherine Milton was executive director of the U.S. program of Save the Children. Her career had revolved around the axiom that service to community is of central importance to a civil, democratic society. The impulse toward service does not, however, come naturally to every citizen; it is a value that must be transmitted from generation to generation. The hows and wherefores of that transmission formed the stable core of Milton's work.

The same idea lay at the core of a long, ramifying series of Wingspread conferences. Milton had attended several of them, and had played an important part in a story that began at Wingspread in 1988.

That July, a group called the Coalition for National Service held a Wingspread conference aimed at establishing a set of strategies "for substantially increasing the number of young people from all walks of life in full-time, year-round, non-sectarian service activities." The 1988 presidential race was just then entering its home stretch as candidates George Bush and Michael Dukakis both jockeyed for a commanding position. A hope often expressed during the National Service conference at Wingspread was that one or both candidates would adopt the idea of voluntary youth service as a campaign theme.

One of the conferees acted on this hope even as the conference took place. Pete McCloskey, a former Republican congressman from California, occasionally slipped out of plenary sessions to make phone calls to Loret Ruppe, a Reagan administration official who was close to Bush, to tell her what was going on at Wingspread. McCloskey urged Ruppe to encourage the Bush people to bring the idea of national youth service into the campaign. She did so.

In Sacramento on October 4, 1988, candidate Bush gave a speech calling for what he called "Youth Engaged in Service—YES to America," a national service foundation. After Bush was elected, Bray and Foundation staff worked closely with the White House "transition team" with the result that Bush's YES to America pledge led eventually to legislation that, in turn, created the Commission on National and Community Service. Its first chairman was Pete McCloskey and one of its members was Catherine Milton.

"The commission members came here, to Wingspread, and met with experts in community service and youth programs," Milton recalled. "We were charged with inventing a new government agency for national service." Eventually, after another presidential campaign and the election of Bill Clinton, the new agency came into being. It was called the Corporation for National Service, and Milton was asked to serve as its first head.

In a note to Bray, McCloskey expressed his view that the events leading to major, bipartisan federal support for youth and community service stemmed directly from the National Service conference held at Wingspread in 1988. "Under the direction of Ellen Porter Honnet, our program consultant, we went on having conferences on youth service," Bray said later. "Wingspread became a kind of an incubator for the idea, an outpost, a place where people could come and wrestle with next steps, exult, get refreshed, then go back again and do the work."

One of The Johnson Foundation's most widely recognized contributions to the field was a set of guidelines for service-based educational programs. The "Principles of Good Practice for Combining Service and Learning," modeled on the earlier "Seven Principles," became *the* universally recognized litmus test for service-learning programs throughout the country.

The "Principles of Good Practice" model proved so powerful that it was emulated again in 1995, this time with an intergenerational spin. A broad-based coalition of sponsors convened a Wingspread conference aimed at developing what became ten "Principles of Good Practice for Building Community Through Lifelong Service and Learning." Early evidence showed that these were not just a set of "clone principles," but a useful and inspiring resource that brought an increasing multigenerational dimension to service-learning programs. Inclusion of the words "building community" in the statement's title helped to capture its central intent.

"We are now focused for the coming years," Bray wrote in a mid-1990s annual report, "on the issues involved in building civil and civic community." The idea of building civil, civic, and (an important added emphasis) *sustainable* communities came to define The Johnson Foundation's vision for its future. It was a vision first

*Conference participants find Wingspread an ideal place to wrestle with new ideas.*

outlined by Samuel C. Johnson, son of H.F. Johnson and one of corporate America's leading environmentalists.

Chairman of SC Johnson & Son as well as the Foundation's board of trustees, Johnson also served on the President's Council on Sustainable Development. As part of the Council, he saw sustainability as a "singular but comprehensive concept" that could shape the activities of the Foundation. Recalling his fond memories of growing up at Wingspread, exploring its ponds and fields, he challenged the Foundation to help assure a healthy environment for coming generations as well. The theme of sustainable community—as timely as it was suggestive—would propel the Foundation beyond the Bray era and into a new millennium.

## "We Did It!"
### Day 3, 1:00 P.M.

*The conferees spent the first half of the final morning of the conference in workgroups, adding details to the group's action plan. The process was still chugging along at the scheduled time for adjournment. At 12:30 P.M., when lunch was supposed to start, the conferees were still pouring heart and soul in the process. Finally, the talking stopped. Members of the group looked at each other. "We did it," someone said.*

*"It feels as if we've accomplished something important," one participant said at lunch. "But we won't know for sure until time has gone by and the items on our action plan start coming to pass. The proof of the pudding's in the eating."*

*Bray had expressed a similar thought two days before when he had welcomed the group to Wingspread. "It's not what happens here that counts," he had told the conferees; "it's what you do back home."*

45

*The Great Hall of Wingspread is light-filled in all seasons.*

# "It All Adds Up"

Shortly after returning to her home in Ann Arbor, Carol Tice sank into an easy chair and sighed. "Wingspread conferences are exhausting," she said. "The intellectual labor is intense. I feel spent. But I also feel exhilarated, grounded, purposeful, and balanced."

The next day, she took a visitor on a drive through Ann Arbor pointing out landmarks that evoked memories of her work. "There's the school where T-LC started," she said. "And here is the middle school where I first met Heather."

The way back to Carol's house led past the University of Michigan campus. "It has one of the top business schools in the country," Carol explained. In addition to involving grandparents, T-LC has a mentoring program on campus too. MBA students volunteer to spend some time each week helping at-risk youths.

"Mentoring can be incredibly important in helping kids make positive choices for their lives," Carol added. "There's Keshia, for example."

Keshia, she explained, had been born to a sixteen-year-old crack addict. Keshia's home environment exhibited nearly every risk factor that would predict a life of anomie and social dependence. Her conduct and school performance during early childhood seemed to fulfill that dire prophecy. Then, at age eleven, Keshia was enrolled in the T-LC MBA Mentors program. The engagement of caring adults in her life seemed to flip some hidden switch. The "real" Keshia began to emerge—bright, articulate, hungry to learn and explore what life had to offer.

At the end of Keshia's second year in the program, her school held a brief ceremony to thank the MBA volunteers. "The Parent-Teacher Organization bought us a maple tree that we planted in the courtyard," Carol recalled. Keshia, who was twelve, gave a brief speech, addressing it to the mentors. "When you are running your corporations," she told them, "I want you to remember this day and this tree. I want you to think about what your decisions mean for this tree and everything it stands for—the land, the earth, this school, and us—the ones you have helped in this program."

Several years later, Keshia's name appeared in news accounts of a Ku Klux Klan rally held in Ann Arbor. Keshia was with a group of counterdemonstrators. Her group converged on a rally spectator who wore a T-shirt emblazoned with a Confederate flag.

The counterdemonstrators began taking out their anger on the man, beating him to the ground. Keshia surged forward and threw her body protectively over the man, shouting, "No more hate." Video footage of the event appeared on national television. Some weeks later, Keshia received an award for distinguished citizenship in New York City.

Asked by a TV reporter what influences led her to act as she did, Keshia immediately cited Carol Tice and her MBA mentors. Carol hands the credit to Wingspread and The Johnson Foundation. "You can't say that any single conference saved Keshia or changed the world," she said, "but you can't deny Wingspread's contribution, either. Without it, I know I couldn't have sustained the vision that has guided my work. And, in the world generally, there would be a significantly smaller force mobilized on behalf of the common good. It all adds up."

*Carl Milles' Angel Musicians pay tribute to Wingspread.*

# ACKNOWLEDGEMENTS

Cover quotation by William B. Boyd,
president emeritus of The Johnson Foundation.

Cover photo of Wingspread by Thomas A. Heinz

**Photo credits:**

Gerald Cross/Imagehaus: pages 36, 38, 44, 47

Samuel H. Gottscho, the Gottscho Collection,
courtesy of the Library of Congress: pages 7, 10,
27, 34, 42

Ray Hartl: pages 11, 16, 36

Thomas A. Heinz: pages 10, 11, 14, 16, 33, 36,
41, 45

The Johnson Foundation archives: pages 15, 16,
18, 21, 22, 28, 30, 31, 33, 40, 41

SC Johnson & Son, Inc.: page 12

**Design & Production:**

Design by Hare Strigenz, Inc., Milwaukee,
Wisconsin

Printed by CastlePierce, Oshkosh, Wisconsin

Printed on Ikono Dull Satin, a 50% recycled
paper by Zanders with 20% post-consumer waste
fiber, processed totally chlorine free. Printed with
soy ink and aqueous coating.

Published by The Johnson Foundation, Inc.,
P.O. Box 547, Racine, Wisconsin 53401-0547.
Copyright © The Johnson Foundation, Inc., 1997.

Printed in the United States of America

The Johnson Foundation's mission is
to help ideas to have consequences
on behalf of the common good.

Our defining idea is community.
We believe that individuals and
their ideas best flourish when
nurtured by others. Those "others"
constitute communities of all kinds,
communities which nurture values,
while nurturing...

THE JOHNSON FOUNDATION, INC.
*Racine, Wisconsin*

ISBN 0-9641794-2-3